MARKETING, SALES & SERVICE

Exploring Career Pathways

Diane Lindsey Reeves

Created and produced by
Bright Futures Press, Cary, North Carolina
www.brightfuturespress.com

Published by
Cherry Lake Publishing, Ann Arbor, Michigan
www.cherrylakepublishing.com

Photo Credits: Cover, Beautyline; page 7, Rawpixel.com, SFIO CRACHO, ESB Professional, Rawpixel.com, cybrain, Micogen, nopporn, Monkey Business Images; page 8, Rawpixel.com; page 10, SFIO CRACHO; page 12, ESB Professional; page 14, Rawpixel.com; page 16, cybrain; page 18, Micogen; page 20, nopporn; page 22, Monkey Business Images; page 24, Sergey Nivens.

Library of Congress Cataloging-in-Publication Date

CIP data has been filed and is available at catalog.loc.gov.

Printed in the United States of America.

TABLE OF CONTENTS

HELLO WORLD OF WORK

This is you.

Right now, your job is to go to school and learn all you can.

This is the world of work.

It's where people earn a living, find purpose in their lives, and make the world a better place.

Sooner or later, you'll have to find your way from

HERE to THERE.

To get started, take all the jobs in the incredibly enormous world of work and organize them into an imaginary pile. It's a big pile, isn't it? It would be pretty tricky to find the perfect job for you among so many options.

No worries!

Some very smart career experts have made it easier to figure out. They sorted jobs and industries into groups by the types of skills and products they share. These groups are called career clusters. They provide pathways that will make it easier for you to find career options that match your interests.

 Architecture & Construction

 Arts & Communication

Business & Administration

Education & Training

Finance

Food & Natural Resources

Government

Health Sciences

Hospitality & Tourism

Human Services

Information Technology

Law & Public Safety

Manufacturing

Marketing, Sales & Service

Science, Technology, Engineering & Mathematics (STEM)

Transportation

Good thing you are still a kid.

You have lots of time to explore ideas and imagine yourself doing all kinds of amazing things. The **World of Work** (WoW for short) series of books will help you get started.

TAKE A HIKE!

There are 16 career pathways waiting for you to explore. The only question is: Which one should you explore first?

Is **Marketing, Sales & Service** a good path for you to start exploring career ideas? There is a lot to like about this pathway. These professionals get the word out about cool new products in ways that cause people to pay attention and buy, buy, buy! They share newsworthy information with the media, and they create memorable brands. They provide great customer service that keeps people coming back for more.

See if any of the following questions grab your interest.

WOULD YOU ENJOY keeping up with the latest fashion trends, picking favorite TV commercials during Super Bowl games, or making posters for a favorite school club?

CAN YOU IMAGINE someday working at an advertising agency, corporate marketing department, or retail store?

ARE YOU CURIOUS ABOUT what creative directors, market researchers, media buyers, retail store managers, and social media consultants do?

If so, it's time to take a hike! Keep reading to see what kinds of opportunities you can discover along the Marketing, Sales & Service pathway.

But wait!

What if you don't think you'll like this pathway?

You have two choices.

You could keep reading, to find out more than you already know. You might be surprised to learn how many amazing careers you'll find along this path.

OR

Turn to page 27 to get ideas about other WoW pathways.

PUBLIC RELATIONS SPECIALIST

CREATIVE DIRECTOR

BRANDING

Innovation

DESIGN   Improving

BRAND MANAGER

STORE MANAGER

MERCHANDISE BUYER

WoW Up Close

They build the brands we love to buy and entice us with memorable marketing messages. They sell products that we want and need and provide helpful customer service and support. These are just some of the important jobs that people who work along the Marketing, Sales & Service pathway do.

SOCIAL MEDIA COORDINATOR

GRAPHIC DESIGNER

MARKET RESEARCH

JANUARY
FEBRUARY

MARKET RESEARCHER

BRAND MANAGER

What kind of sneakers are you wearing? What kind of chips do you like best? Where do you go when you crave a cheeseburger and fries? Your answers to these questions share something in common. They are all brands. A brand is the name of a specific product made by a specific company.

When **brand managers** do a good job, it is the name that comes to mind when you think of a certain type of product.

Think cola. What comes to mind? Coke or Pepsi? Think burger. Does McDonald's or Wendy's come to mind first?

Brand managers are in charge of a specific product within a company that may sell lots of products. Their job is to do whatever it takes to get people to recognize, buy, and enjoy that product.

Imagine you are the brand manager for a new chocolate candy bar. You might start building the brand by picking the perfect name and creating a **logo** for the product. You will do lots of research about pricing it and identifying the type of person most likely to buy it. You'll work on packaging the product in a way that will make it stand out among all the other candy bars on the grocery shelves. You'll be involved in putting together promotions that might include magazine ads, TV commercials, and a cool online game.

Needless to say, the job involves good business sense and lots of creativity.

Check It Out!

Explore famous brands at

▶ http://bit.ly/BrandNames1

Start Now!

- ✔ Make a matching game with logos from popular brands. See if your friends and family can match the logo with its brand name.

- ✔ Pick a favorite product and create a poster that is sure to get people to notice it.

- ✔ Design a logo for a brand you'd like to manage someday.

CREATIVE DIRECTOR

The creative department of an ad agency is a busy place. It's where marketing commercials, materials, and campaigns are created. Imaginative ideas come at a fast pace as creative people **brainstorm** ways to make the most of each marketing opportunity. It is up to the **creative director** to round up all those ideas and turn them into spectacular marketing plans.

Creative directors work with all kinds of talented people, including designers, artists, copywriters, and producers. They also work with each client's sales team and marketing manager. Sometimes their job puts them in a bit of a "monkey in the middle" position—they have to make sure their creative team's ideas are in line with their client's expectations. It is their job to keep everyone happy and working together in productive ways.

Creative directors spend a lot of time planning and managing other people. They are good leaders. They not only have good ideas themselves but also know how to draw out the best ideas from others. Creative directors learn to thrive in a fast-paced environment where many people work on many projects at the same time. They learn how to give and receive gentle criticism. This helps them create marketing materials that grab attention and convince consumers that they need or want the product being promoted.

Check It Out!

Search online for "best commercials of all time" to find examples of successful creative directors' work.

Start Now!

- ✓ Create **storyboards** for a commercial selling a favorite (or imaginary) product you think kids your age would like to buy.

- ✓ Volunteer to make posters for a school club or activity.

- ✓ Look through some of the catalogs that come in your family's mail to see how different companies promote their products.

GRAPHIC DESIGNER

Notice how this chapter features an image of a graphic designer, a big bold headline, and colorful text boxes? A creative **graphic designer** named Chris made those design decisions to make this book as fun to look at as it is to read.

Graphic designers are tech-**savvy** artists who create attention-grabbing magazines, books, brochures, posters, ads, Web sites, and more. They use color, special typefaces called **fonts**, illustrations, images, and lots of creativity to produce marketing materials that make their clients look good in print.

Graphic design is used to give businesses a distinct identity that customers easily recognize whenever they see it. Think golden arches and how people around the world immediately connect that logo with McDonald's. That is the power of good graphic design.

One of the challenges of the job is matching the right look with the right company. After all, a poster for a senior citizens' community would require a different approach than one for a children's toy store. One would need to look a bit more grown-up than the other, don't you think?

Graphic designers use special computer programs to work their artistic magic. Some work in-house in publishing companies or ad agencies. Others work for design firms or run their own small business.

Check It Out!

Look at award-winning graphic designs at

▶ https://www.awwwards.com

▶ http://bit.ly/GDPrizes

Start Now!

- ✓ Sketch out some of your creative ideas at https://scratch.mit.edu.

- ✓ Print out a page with your name written in a variety of different fonts.

- ✓ Make posters to promote a school or community event.

MARKET RESEARCHER

Chances are your parents have a card that is scanned at the checkout counter of the grocery store. Your parents love it because it saves money off the price of certain items they are buying. **Market researchers** love it because it provides lots of data about the types of products your parents like to buy.

In fact, market researchers know a lot about you and your family. From your favorite brand of toilet paper to the type of car you own, the information they collect helps companies make decisions about the types of products to make and sell.

Market researchers use a variety of tools to gain this information. Their goal is to find out as much as possible about who buys what. The information they gather is called **demographics**, and it paints a very detailed picture about a product's ideal customers. How old are they? Are they male or female? Do they live in suburban or urban areas? What is their education level? This type of information helps businesses come up with marketing plans that reach the people most likely to buy their products.

A college degree in market research, statistics, or business administration prepares a market researcher to work with all the numbers and data required in the job. People skills are a must, too. Understanding **human behavior** helps them explain what the numbers mean.

Check It Out!

Look into how market research works at

- http://bit.ly/MarketReseach1
- http://bit.ly/MarketResearch2

Start Now!

- Conduct a survey to find out which cafeteria meals your classmates like most.

- Get a **focus group** of friends together to talk about your favorite series of books. Ask questions about what they like and dislike about these books.

- Pick a favorite brand of clothes and make a list of the types of people most likely to wear them.

MERCHANDISE BUYER

Walk into any big department store and you will find they all share one thing in common. They sell lots and lots of products! Before those products arrive in stores for people to buy, a **merchandise buyer** buys them for the store to sell.

If you think it sounds like merchandisers do a lot of shopping, you are correct. Everything from toothpaste and toys to designer clothes and lawn furniture has been carefully selected to appeal to the types of customers who shop at that store. Merchandise buyers track down the perfect products by doing market research, attending trade shows, meeting with **vendors**, and consulting catalogs. Sometimes they work with designers to create new products that are made to sell only in their stores.

Good buyers need common sense and good instincts. Even after collecting all the necessary data, they have to make educated guesses about the types of products their customers want or need. They have to stay on top of trends to be prepared with "hot" new products. They have to keep certain types of products around at certain times of the year, like Valentine's candy or back-to-school supplies.

Some of these skills only come with on-the-job training and experience. Other skills come from earning a college degree in merchandising or business management.

Check It Out!

Explore what merchandise buyers do at

▶ http://bit.ly/MerchBuyer1

▶ http://bit.ly/MerchBuyer2

Start Now!

✓ Create a catalog of products you'd like to find in a favorite shop. Make sketches and go online and print out pictures of products you would want to buy.

✓ The next time you visit a grocery store, notice how many different brands of soap are sold. Try to imagine how different brands would appeal to different types of customers.

✓ Make a list of the top fashion trends at your school.

PUBLIC RELATIONS SPECIALIST

Public relations (PR) specialists are the link between a business with news to share and the media that shares the news with the public. Their job is to keep people informed about their company's good—and bad—news about products, programs, and projects and other newsworthy events.

Writing is a big part of the PR specialists' job. They write press releases that provide accurate information and images to the media. They write newsletters, blogs, and tweets to keep their company's name in front of the public. They also conduct **press briefings** and must keep their cool and represent their company well while under pressure and in the spotlight.

Of course, this job is more fun when there is good news to share. There is a special art to sharing bad news, but it is important to be up-front and honest about what's going on. People might get mad when a product fails or injures someone, but trying to hide problems like that can ruin a business. Once trust is broken, it's hard to rebuild it, no matter how good the PR efforts may be.

One of the most famous, and often most difficult, PR jobs is that of press secretary for a political figure. This person must stand in front of a roomful of reporters and cameras to explain the policies of the politician he or she represents. The tough questions come fast and furiously, and this PR specialist must be prepared to respond with lots of facts without getting flustered.

Check It Out!

Find out how to write a press release at

▶ http://bit.ly/PressStudents

Explore how PR works at

▶ http://bit.ly/PRWorks

Start Now!

- ✔ Write a press release about a big school or community event. Be sure to include all the who, what, when, where, and how details!

- ✔ Make a list of snappy headlines to describe your favorite TV show or musician.

SOCIAL MEDIA COORDINATOR

Social media is a big—make that huge—new tool in the marketing tool kit. There are Web sites, Facebook, and Instagram. LinkedIn, Twitter, Pinterest, and YouTube, too. Technology keeps making it easier for businesses to reach their target audiences. But with so many options, it's tricky to know the best tools to use.

Figuring out how to use the right social media tools to reach a company's customers is what **social media coordinators** do. First, they have to find out where their customers hang out online. Then they have to craft messages to reach them through posts, videos, tweets, blogs, and more.

The really tricky part of social media is that social media coordinators can't just blast out ads that say, "Buy my products!" They have to be creative in finding ways to connect with their audience in ways that gets people's attention and gains their respect.

Social media coordinators are whizzes at using the latest technologies. However, they have to compete with everyone and their brother to get their customers' attention. That's why they concern themselves with things like **search engine optimization** to make sure their messages make it through the clatter of all the other social media.

There are lots of ways to learn about social media. A college degree is one route. But the learning never ends as coordinators must keep up with the latest social media platforms.

Check It Out!

Learn about how to stay safe online at

▶ http://pbskids.org/webonauts

▶ http://www.safekids.com

Start Now!

✓ Write a blog or create a poster describing what you learned about online safety.

✓ Create a "tweet" to share the best news of your day in 140 characters (that's letters and spaces) or less.

✓ Pick a favorite store or brand, and go to their Web site to see how they use social media to touch base with customers like you.

STORE MANAGER

Someone has to be in charge of the sales, staff, and stock at every store you shop in. That someone is the **store manager**. Store managers are in charge of the day-to-day operations of a store. It is their job to do what it takes to make sure that customers have a good experience when shopping at their store.

There are many things to take care of, so being super organized is a good thing for store managers. Their workday often starts before the doors open for business. They must make sure that the store is clean, shelves are stocked with products, cash registers are up and running, and enough staff is scheduled to run the store. Sometimes their days extend beyond the time their store closes. That's when they conduct staff training sessions, process new **inventory**, and handle **payroll**.

Good people skills are an absolute must for this job. Store managers must be good leaders and able to manage their employees. They must also provide excellent customer service—even when customers get difficult. You know what they say: "The customer is always right."

A college degree is not always necessary to become a store manager. Some managers get on-the-training and move up the ranks as they get experience working in stores.

Check It Out!

Go online to visit the Web site of your favorite store. Notice the differences between an online and in-person shopping experience.

Start Now!

- Make a list of all the stores you pass on the way from your home to your school.

- Volunteer to help out the next time your family has a yard sale. You can help tag items with prices, set up the items for sale, and help customers with purchases.

- Visit two different stores that sell the same type of product (like shoes, for instance). See if you can spot at least five things that make each store unique.

Administrative assistant • Advertising director • Advertising sales manager • Analyst • Applications developer • Assessor • Assistant store manager • Brand ambassador • **BRAND MANAGER** • Bridal consultant • Business development specialist • Cashier • Channel supervisor • Checker • Client services manager • Communications director • Computer programmer • **CREATIVE DIRECTOR** • Crew member • Customer service associate • Customer service representative • Delivery driver • Demonstration specialist • Department manager • Design consultant • Director of online strategy • Display decorator • E-commerce entrepreneur • E-commerce marketing

WoW Big List

Take a look at some of the different kinds of jobs people do in the Marketing, Sales & Service pathway. **WoW!**

Some of these job titles will be familiar to you. Others will be so unfamiliar that you will scratch your head and say "huh?"

manager • Event coordinator • Fashion designer • Field interviewer • Field merchandiser • Floral designer • Florist • Food demonstrator • Front services representative • Fulfillment representative • **GRAPHIC DESIGNER** • Guest services agent • Independent beauty consultant • Independent distributor • In-store marketing associate • Interior designer • Internet programmer • Inventory and pricing associate • Leasing consultant • Market

analyst • Marketing clerk • Marketing director • **MARKET RESEARCHER**
• Market survey representative • Media buyer • **MERCHANDISE BUYER**
• Merchandise manager • Office assistant • Office manager • Online
marketing manager • Online service manager • Parking attendant • Product
line manager • Product manager • Project manager • Promotions manager
• Property manager • **PUBLIC RELATIONS SPECIALIST** • Real estate
agent • Real estate appraiser • Real estate assessor • Real estate broker •
Receptionist • Rental agent • Residence manager • Retail advertising sales
manager • Retail buyer • Sales associate • Sales clerk • Sales engineer •

Find a job title that makes you curious. Type the name of the job into your
favorite Internet search engine and find out more about the people who
have that job.

1 What do they do?

2 Where do they work?

3 How much training do they need to do this job?

Sales representative • Sales route driver • Scan coordinator • Search engine
optimization (SEO) director • Secretary • Shift manager • **SOCIAL MEDIA
COORDINATOR** • Software developer • Stocker • Stockroom clerk • **STORE
MANAGER** • Street vendor • Study director • Telemarketer • Toll collector
• Trader • Valet • Valuation Consultant • Visual merchandiser • Warehouse
pricing and inventory clerk • Wedding planner • Wholesale representative

TAKE YOUR PICK

	Put stars next to your 3 favorite career ideas	Put an X next to the career idea you like the least	Put a question mark next to the career idea you want to learn more about
Brand manager			
Creative director			
Graphic designer			
Market researcher			
Merchandise buyer			
Public relations specialist			
Social media coordinator			
Store manager			

	What do you like most about these careers?	What is it about this career that doesn't appeal to you?	What do you want to learn about this career? Where can you find answers?

Which Big Wow List ideas are you curious about?

EXPLORE SOME MORE

The Marketing, Sales & Service pathway is only one of 16 career pathways that hold exciting options for your future. Take a look at the other 15 to figure out where to start exploring next.

 ## Architecture & Construction

WOULD YOU ENJOY making things with LEGOs™, building a treehouse or birdhouse, or designing the world's best skate park?

CAN YOU IMAGINE someday working at a construction site, a design firm, or a building company?

ARE YOU CURIOUS ABOUT what civil engineers, demolition technicians, heavy-equipment operators, landscape architects, or urban planners do?

 ## Arts & Communication

WOULD YOU ENJOY drawing your own cartoons, using your smartphone to make a movie, or writing articles for the student newspaper?

CAN YOU IMAGINE someday working at a Hollywood movie studio, a publishing company, or a television news station?

ARE YOU CURIOUS ABOUT what actors, bloggers, graphic designers, museum curators, or writers do?

 ## Business & Administration

WOULD YOU ENJOY playing Monopoly, being the boss of your favorite club or team, or starting your own business?

CAN YOU IMAGINE someday working at a big corporate headquarters, government agency, or international business center?

ARE YOU CURIOUS ABOUT what brand managers, chief executive officers, e-commerce analysts, entrepreneurs, or purchasing agents do?

 ## Education & Training

WOULD YOU ENJOY babysitting, teaching your grandparents how to use a computer, or running a summer camp for neighbor kids in your backyard?

CAN YOU IMAGINE someday working at a college counseling center, corporate training center, or school?

ARE YOU CURIOUS ABOUT what animal trainers, coaches, college professors, guidance counselors, or principals do?

 **Finance**

WOULD YOU ENJOY earning and saving money, being the class treasurer, or playing the stock market game?

CAN YOU IMAGINE someday working at an accounting firm, bank, or Wall Street stock exchange?

ARE YOU CURIOUS ABOUT what accountants, bankers, fraud investigators, property managers, or stockbrokers do?

 Food & Natural Resources

WOULD YOU ENJOY exploring nature, growing your own garden, or setting up a recycling center at your school?

CAN YOU IMAGINE someday working at a national park, raising crops in a city farm, or studying food in a laboratory?

ARE YOU CURIOUS ABOUT what landscape architects, chefs, food scientists, environmental engineers, or forest rangers do?

 Government

WOULD YOU ENJOY reading about U.S. presidents, running for student council, or helping a favorite candidate win an election?

CAN YOU IMAGINE someday working at a chamber of commerce, government agency, or law firm?

ARE YOU CURIOUS about what mayors, customs agents, federal special agents, intelligence analysts, or politicians do?

 Health Sciences

WOULD YOU ENJOY nursing a sick pet back to health, dissecting animals in a science lab, or helping the school coach run a sports clinic?

CAN YOU IMAGINE someday working at a dental office, hospital, or veterinary clinic?

ARE YOU CURIOUS ABOUT what art therapists, doctors, dentists, pharmacists, and veterinarians do?

 Hospitality & Tourism

WOULD YOU ENJOY traveling, sightseeing, or meeting people from other countries?

CAN YOU IMAGINE someday working at a convention center, resort, or travel agency?

ARE YOU CURIOUS ABOUT what convention planners, golf pros, tour guides, resort managers, or wedding planners do?

 Human Services

WOULD YOU ENJOY showing a new kid around your school, organizing a neighborhood food drive, or being a peer mediator?

CAN YOU IMAGINE someday working at an elder care center, fitness center, or mental health center?

ARE YOU CURIOUS ABOUT what elder care center directors, hairstylists, personal trainers, psychologists, or religious leaders do?

Information Technology

WOULD YOU ENJOY creating your own video game, setting up a Web site, or building your own computer?

CAN YOU IMAGINE someday working at an information technology start-up company, software design firm, or research and development laboratory?

ARE YOU CURIOUS ABOUT what artificial intelligence scientists, big data analysts, computer forensic investigators, software engineers, or video game designers do?

Law & Public Safety

WOULD YOU ENJOY working on the school safety patrol, participating in a mock court trial at school, or coming up with a fire escape plan for your home?

CAN YOU IMAGINE someday working at a cyber security company, fire station, police department, or prison?

ARE YOU CURIOUS ABOUT what animal control officers, coroners, detectives, firefighters, or park rangers do?

Manufacturing

WOULD YOU ENJOY figuring out how things are made, competing in a robot-building contest, or putting model airplanes together?

CAN YOU IMAGINE someday working at a high-tech manufacturing plant, engineering firm, or global logistics company?

ARE YOU CURIOUS ABOUT what chemical engineers, industrial designers, supply chain managers, robotics technologists, or welders do?

Science, Technology, Engineering & Mathematics (STEM)

WOULD YOU ENJOY concocting experiments in a science lab, trying out the latest smartphone, or taking advanced math classes?

CAN YOU IMAGINE someday working in a science laboratory, engineering firm, or research and development center?

ARE YOU CURIOUS ABOUT what aeronautical engineers, ecologists, statisticians, oceanographers, or zoologists do?

Transportation

WOULD YOU ENJOY taking pilot or sailing lessons, watching a NASA rocket launch, or helping out in the school carpool lane?

CAN YOU IMAGINE someday working at an airport, mass transit system, or shipping port?

ARE YOU CURIOUS ABOUT what air traffic controllers, flight attendants, logistics planners, surveyors, and traffic engineers do?

MY WoW

I am here.

Name

Grade

School

Who I am.

Make a word collage! Use 5 adjectives to form a picture that describes who you are.

Where I'm going.

The next career pathway I want to explore is

Some things I need to learn first to succeed.

1

2

3

My Career Choice

To get here.

GLOSSARY

brainstorm
a process where a group of people suggest lots of ideas for a future activity or project

brand manager
person who uses marketing strategies to make a product more popular

creative director
person in charge of a design firm, design department, or ad agency

demographics
characteristics of human populations and population segments used to identify consumer markets

focus group
a diverse group of people who take part in a guided discussion about a specific topic or product

fonts
styles of type

inventory
all the items on hand for sale in a store

graphic designer
person who combines images, words, and ideas to convey information to an audience

human behavior
the full range of physical and emotional behaviors that humans engage in

logo
a symbol or graphic used to represent a product

market researcher
person who gathers, analyzes, and explains information about buyers' needs and preferences

merchandise buyer
person who decides which products are sold in stores and online

payroll
a list of workers who are paid by a company, along with the amount each is to be paid

press briefings
media events in which newsmakers invite journalists to hear them speak and ask questions about events, products, or other newsworthy information

public relations specialist
person who creates and maintains a favorable public image for the organization he or she represents

savvy
practical know-how

search engine optimization
the name given to the activity that improves a Web site's visibility [OR ranking] when someone does a search related to what that site offers

social media coordinator
person who helps a business increase its online presence; build buzz for a new product, service, or company; and convert that buzz into profit

store manager
person responsible for the day-to-day operations of a retail business

storyboards
series of drawings or images showing the planned order of a commercial, story, movie, or other creative project

vendors
people or companies offering something for sale

INDEX

* Refers to the Web page sources

About the Author

Diane Lindsey Reeves is the author of lots of children's books. She has written several original PEANUTS stories (published by Regnery Kids and Sourcebooks). She is especially curious about what people do and likes to write books that get kids thinking about all the cool things they can be when they grow up. She lives in Cary, North Carolina, and her favorite thing to do is play with her grandkids—Conrad, Evan, Reid, and Hollis Grace.